After Giotto

Giotto was the first artist
to depict the human face
in a natural and realistic way –
changing European art for ever

After Giotto

Heather Scott

Edited by Joy Hendry

Chapman

2023

Chapman
4 Broughton Place
Edinburgh
EH1 3RX
Scotland
First published 2023

A catalogue record for this volume is available from the British Library.

ISBN 978-1-903700-22-8

Cover illustration by Geoffrey Roper
Photograph by Gordon Miller

Heather Scott photograph by Tim Porter

Typeset in Goudy Old Style by Chapman
and Leamington Books

Printed by Severn, Gloucester

Contents

Foreword

After Giotto is the first and only book of poetry by Heather Scott. That there have been no more is a loss to us all. She was a poet of talent and skill, tackling a wide range of subjects, and variety of forms, styles and modes. She could have been an important poet decades ago. An early poem, 'The Top Board', published in her school magazine, reveals a knowing self-confidence: she happily rejects diving from on high as a goal worth pursuing. Aged only 15, she already has an easy command of poetic form – and an individuality of mind which has all the hallmarkings of a poet.

Like many women partnered with men successful in one field or another, she allowed the vocation of her husband, Tom Scott, to take priority. As the family breadwinner, her work-load had been onerous, but it was her attitude too. On seeing poetry she'd written in the 1980s, I tried to encourage her to write much more: she rounded on me and said, quite firmly: "I think one poet in the family is one too many."

After he died, in 1995, she began to write more poetry herself, put energy into getting published – and continued her learning of languages, and translating, especially Italian.

She's in fine company in this – Willa Muir, Valda Grieve – so many women have done exactly this, but the world is a poorer place for it. Thankfully, now, most women see tending their own abilities as a duty, even an inalienable right. She was reluctant to take herself seriously as a poet right up to the end. When I first proposed this book, in 2019, she was incredulous, thinking herself unworthy even to approach Richard Berengarten to write an introduction. But she soon warmed to the whole idea, and was looking forward to seeing published. It is one of my greatest regrets that she died before this could happen, on 24 August 2021.

7

She did live to see and approve most of the poems and translations here. I have made only minor editorial changes, and when it became clear she might not be able to oversee all, she gave me *carte blanche* to use my own judgement – her own came finely honed and tuned. I have done this as little as possible – the most significant change being to alter the incidents described in the title poem 'After Giotto' from past to present tense. I have also expanded the translation section; if anything, she gave higher priority to this work than to writing more from her own voice and persona – reticence again, I suspect.

Shortly before she died, I was able to visit Edinburgh Royal Infirmary late at night, to put into her hands a fine copy of the inside book. She herself chose the mysterious and provocative cover image in the painting by Geoffrey Roper, which hung on her living room wall, opposite her habitual chair. Over the next four or five days, her bairns, Eric, Kim and Marina read her poems out to her, though we will never know how aware she was of what was happening, or if she could hear her own words ringing out.

Many people have helped in creating this book: all the family, Elisabetta Perosino of the Italian Institute in Edinburgh, Colin Donati, Richard Berengarten, Gordon Miller, Rosario Alejandra, Mira Knoche, Malcolm Hughes, Joe Farrell, Peter Burnett, – and all the commentators at the end of the book – to all of them, and more, my thanks for their support and encouragement.

Heather Scott was a good poet 'in her own write', a wonderful friend to me and many others, and a very fine human being.

Joy Hendry

Tending, Attending

All her life, Heather Scott has lived in the homeland of poetry. For many years, she's been well known in poetry circles, especially in Edinburgh, as a keenly attentive reader, as a translator from Italian, and as a loyal friend, supporter, and defender of poets. Now, from these pages, we discover that all along she has been a gifted poet herself, working away in a typically quiet, modest, unassuming and reticent way, to produce this extraordinary gathering of poems.

I deploy words like "quiet, modest, unassuming, reticent" and combine them with "extraordinary" entirely advisedly. What I mean is that the resonant quality of Heather Scott's poems is no loud, shouting matter, and that a second reading, and more, will gradually reveal their depths, insights, their integrity and her passionate accuracy. For one thing, her language at all times flows across a conversational surface that's both intimate and transparent, never calling special attention to itself. To extend Wordsworth's claim in his 'Preface to Lyrical Ballads', here genuinely is "language, such as men" and women "do use". For another, Heather Scott's poetic vision is both piercingly sharp and subtly gentle, and her craft, at once lucid and mysterious. It's lucid, thanks to the careful clarity and caring precision of her language, in both English and Scots; and it's mysterious, because it shares an acute awareness that while the hems and rims of our mortal condition require our full attention, the precise conditions of their ever-fraying edges and borders can never be entirely within our command, since our little life is rounded with a sleep.

In this book, a reader will find glimpses and depictions of a rich personal world, spanning human life from birth and childhood to old age and death, ranging from memories of a tree "planted by the door / on the day that I was born" ('My Tree'), to waiting for "the footstep" placed "on the stair" by that strange, but familiar 'Visitor' who must eventually call on each and every one of us. Between these edges and borders of knowing reside rich insights into moments of sadness, poignancy and pain, and equally, of grace and beauty. Envisionings such as these – which belong ineluctably to the present, to presence – often arrive, wryly and eerily, in each other's intimate company, for like John Keats, Heather Scott knows that "Ay, in the very temple of delight / Veil'd Melancholy has her sovran shrine."

Heather Scott's poems are always rooted in richly felt personal experience, from memories of her childhood in an English 'Dormitory Suburb, Surrey, 1950', to the memorial poem for her brother Colin, which is permeated with "a spread of golden roses" ('The Visiting Hour'). Nothing here is merely self-expressive. Poems ostensibly about herself, for example 'On Not Having Grandchildren', reach, simply and quietly, *through* subjectivity, down into transpersonal (i.e. archetypal) layers. So, while every poem is generated, governed and authenticated by experience, many other people appear too: for example, a Jewish Holocaust survivor with a "number tattooed on her pale arm" ('After Giotto'); a Muslim friend who commits suicide because "he no longer had / a Homeland" ('In Memoriam'); a "Celtic hermit in his cell" ('Contentment'); Father Colum ('Iona'); and Isa in her shop on St Stephen's Street ('Brief Reflections on a Pregnancy'). Nor, clearly, is this poetic world insular, it is genuinely international; and nor is it occupied only by humans. Other living creatures abound too: for example, 'The Fox'; a 'Donkey, Seen on TV during the Balkans War'; and a "pair of swans" on 'The Lake at Dawn', reminding me (for one) of the "swan in the evening" in the beautiful Irish song 'She Moved through the Fair'. As this short list suggests, this book is infused with a quietly empowering sense of the preciousness and fragility of life, flowing through an ecology of thought and feeling.

All this is to say that, at every level and in every direction, Heather Scott's poems embody otherness, include others. Consider, for example, the lines:

> Who caused the young squaddy
> to die of leukaemia?
> "Not us," said the War Lords
> for justice in Whitehall's smooth fortress.
>
> (WHODUNNIT ?)

and compare these with Sorley MacLean's translation of his own Second World War poem, 'Curaidhean' ('Heroes'), in which he laments the death of another lad, another squaddy, in the North African desert:

> [a] poor little chap with chubby cheeks
> and knees grinding each other,
> pimply unattractive face –
> garment of the bravest spirit.

In both poets, dignity and respect for the other is the key. In both, there dwells an unvarnished and compassionate humanness, stamped with a blessed rage at the injustices and stupidities perpetrated by fools in power. Yet, permeating all this is the fullest possible sense of the miraculously unique quality, the extraordinariness of every person, creature and thing – even if the entity might at first glance seem no more than ordinary, humdrum, easy to pass over or pass by. This, I believe, is the quality of the *common miracle*. It's a quality that doesn't shout but speaks to the heart, quietly and caringly. And this quality is precisely that *sine qua non*, without-which no poet can genuinely touch and move a reader. Its name is *magnanimity, weel-hertitness, fialaidheachd, megalopsychia, velikodušnost* – and it is universal. Heather Scott's poems tend and attend this quality: they attend to it, pay attention to it, attend on it.

For all these reasons, it's a twin pleasure and privilege to have been given these exquisite, strong, beautiful poems by Joy Hendry, and to have been invited to preface them. And while I know that these few words don't do Heather Scott's poems full justice, I hope they'll at least whet an appetite or two among poetry lovers hungry for the real thing.

Richard Berengarten

Me? A Poet?

I do not write –
I do not want to write
of granny's kettle singing on the hob,
the hills of home, or my first love.

Wilder themes insist on being heard:
the ocean's pull, the swing of stars
that fling philosophies aside;
human folly, human woes
that clamour for concern;
the suffering planet
that beats a warning drum
which, for life's sake
cannot be ignored.

And yet, and yet
how deep in memory the kettle sings,
and still, and stronger still,
what pain
the memory of first love brings.

Voyage of Discovery

Meantime he had found amongst the rubbish in one of the empty rooms a notebook belonging to the old adventurer. He studied the crabbed handwriting of its pages and often grew meditative over it.

             – Joseph Conrad

Its cracked leather binding, salt-stained,
crabbed writing fading on a dampened page,
the tight, unfaltering hand in browning ink,
hundreds of close-packed lines
making a dense whole –
you hold the journal as the thing it is,
but read, if you can –
it's worth deciphering . . .

Through the seaweed tangle of the words
glimpse secret oceans, untravelled shores,
dark-caverned cliffs and emerald lagoons,
pearl strewn strands
curled shells and conches,
mermaid-haunted rocks;
storms and calms
and monsters of the deep
and great stars guiding the ship herself,
loved like a woman,
her spreading sails milk-white beneath the moon
as she sets forth
upon her greatest enterprise.

Birthright

I began in a cry of love
and was born in a cry of pain,
and between these moments swam
through all the ages known to man.
Cradled in a warm sea
I floated, dreamed, absorbed
the memories of him and her,
of her and him since time began,
that knowledge running like a fuse
through my growing flesh and bone and vein.

In my veins runs the blood
of the peasant and the artisan,
hunter, soldier, poet, nurse,
builder, weaver, courtesan.
I danced my way across the earth,
I learned the secrets of the sea and land,
clay and metal were moulded by my hand.
I was mother, father, child,
familiar with town and forest, shore and field.

All this I dreamed and learned
while growing beneath her heart
and cherished by his hand;
bound to them both
by the thread of choice or chance
that through the ages runs
towards the tiny mystery
of my own making.

Dormitory Suburb, Surrey, 1950

Raynes Park, Motspur Park, Worcester Park,
Stoneleigh - all stations to Effingham Junction!
The shouted litany of the Southern Line
as, coming home from school each day,
I leaned my cheek against the pane
and saw the long back gardens pass
all different and all the same.
French windows, garden ponds and washing lines,
privet and trellis screening each from each.

At Worcester Park, the long walk home,
past neat front garden, rockery and gnome,
past pillar-box and regimented tree,
and Mrs Dale from every open window
- loud and clear.

With pigtails, long white socks and cotton gloves
and heavy schoolbag bumping at my side
I trailed up Balmoral Road
towards a bread and marmite tea.

But if the Tudor gables mocked me as I passed,
I didn't care, because they didn't know
it wasn't a lumpy schoolgirl walking there -
but Juliette Gréco tossing back her long black hair.

My Tree

A tree was planted by the door
on the day that I was born.

We grew together,
and for some years my fingertips
met around its trunk.

Better than a friend,
it was a playmate when I climbed
and always shook with laughter
at my jokes.

It heard my secrets,
sheltered me,
and sometimes dried my tears
with its cool leaves.

But now a strange bird
has landed on my tree
and fingers stretch in vain to touch.

I wait with beating heart
to feel its claws.

Brief Reflections on a Pregnancy
Edinburgh, 1964

"It's twins," the doctor briskly said,
tapping the X-rays with his pen.
"No home delivery for you, my lass –
We'll book you into Simpson's
right away."

Dazed, I wandered home.
In Howe Street met Olivia,
the Professor's wife –
Told her my news.

"How wonderful my dear," she gushed.
"How lovely for you.
You'll have such fun
dressing them alike –
if it's girls, of course."
And, beaming,
she pedalled away.

That night, needing carrots and bread,
I trudged down St Stephen's Street
And into Isa's shop.
"You're lookin' tired, hen," she said.
"It's twins," I said.
Isa put down her knitting.

"Aw, whit a damn shame –
Ah'm awfae sorry hen," she said.

The Minoans

Fearing no enemies
they built their palaces
without defensive walls
on sun-drenched hilltops
or beside the turquoise sea,
with deep cool cisterns
of fresh water from the rocks
and store-rooms holding jars
of grain and oil and wine.

Their gods were gods of nature,
birds and trees, the hills, the sea,
and they did not bow down to them
but showed their reverence standing
with arms outstretched
or folded across their breast.
Their shrines were topped with doves
their tributes baskets full of flowers.

The women were graceful
bare of breast with tiny waists
their long black ringlets piled high
wearing bracelets and earrings made of gold
pendants of golden butterflies or bees
and wide skirts hiding little feet.

The young men raced and wrestled
the maidens danced together in a ring.
Boys and girls would leap the bull
risking in sport the wounds
no battle would ever bring.
Weapons they had, but finely made, exquisite.
clearly meant for ritual not war.

A peaceful people.

How did it end, this Eden,
three thousand years ago?

One day the whole earth shook
as nearby Santorini atomised.
The blue sky thickened, turning sulphur-black
the sea drew back and left the fishes
                        gasping on the sand
then rushed back in again with a hideous roar –
a mountain of water
swallowing people and cattle,
olive grove and vine
engulfing palaces and plains
and then receded,
leaving only piles of stones,
a culture buried in the sand,
and on the hilltops
sea-shells scattered as on a shore.

•

Lexis

We fumble in the dark with words worn smooth
which all day long have passed from use to use,
like grubby coins spent buying vegetables,
tags with knock-down prices hawking rubbish,
capering on paper, scrawled on walls,
or advertising soap.
And in the dark they do not mean
the things we want to say,
or else, their value shifting, mean too much.

And even if we crossed a poet's palm with silver,
could he make us bright new words
to play with or to spend?
Or have we reached the country of the riddle,
where the natives cannot tell the truth,
and we, the travellers,
can only deal in silence or in lies?

Fremmit

The track gaes naewhaur nou
– naewhaur but a rickle o stanes,
a cauld hairth owregrown,
welcome tae nane but the moupin sheep;
an amang the strewn wrack o a gavel-end
the laverock maks her nest
in a hassock o gress.

An gane are the bairns that yince
ran owre the bents tae skuil
or gied their daddie a haun
wi the boatie on the sea-loch.

But mony's the chiel
frae Calgary or Delaware
stauns there an hears
or fancies that he hears
the cries o bairnies
cairriet i the wind.

Magdalene

I tried to thank him
every way I knew.
I washed his feet with tears
and dried them with my hair.
But it was not enough.

I tried to warn him what men are –
what cruelties their guilt can lead them to
– of course I tried.

He smiled.
He only smiled.
His innocence was round him like a flame.

I anointed him with oil
and wanted him to take a sword and be a king –
but he took bread and blessed it.

Right from the start I knew,
of course I knew,
one night they'd come for him.

And now he's gone
And all the world's askew
And all the world can never be enough.

Iona

Father Colum, where have you brought us?
This isle is bleak and bare, the wind is cold.

    See, brother, the Lord has given us stones
    so we may build our shelter.

But Father, the sea is salt,
our flasks are dry
our thirst is great.

    Seek a little further, brothers
    and you shall find sweet water in the rocks.

Father, there is only windswept grass
beyond the sand
from bay to bay.

    Brothers, look again, the grass is starred
    with flowers
    and where they grow so may the grain,
    and for our present need
    the Lord has given us fish
    that teem beside the shore.

Father, in this place we see no man,
nor maid, nor child.
How then shall we speak
God's holy word, and teach?

Patience, brothers, for men shall come,
numberless as grains of sand,
and in this place of earth glimpse heaven
and through their humble faith be shriven
white as the stones upon this beach.

Contentment

A Celtic hermit in his cell
working by sunlight
working by rushlight
spent his days and years
writing the lives of saints.

His companion was his cat.
They did not speak a lot
but when they did
their words were loving.

Each had his task:
the hermit had to write,
the cat caught mice.
The lives of saints like mice
ran quickly across the page.

As for the mice,
their lives were brief.
Hermit and cat,
each knew his place,
and when they slept
they dreamed together
of prisoner mice
and captured saints.

A Nation of Shopkeepers?

Along the High Street
there's a string of shops –
good causes all –
some brightly lit and smart
others a dingy jumble,
for charity has its hierarchy it seems.

Inside women jostle
among cast-off clothing, cast-off lives,
hoping to spot a bargain
and hoping too, perhaps,
their pennies might help some poor soul
or go towards a need
that governments won't touch.

Dealers too survey the shelves
hoping to make a bob or two
from someone's treasure, someone's trash.

Tasselled lampshades, faded prints,
teapots and trinkets,
souvenirs from Spain –
the pride of many a mantelpiece
is pushed to the back of a crowded shelf.

And outside on the pavement
stands a cardboard box of books
marked "All at twenty pence".

A mildewed Shakespeare,
The Wonder Book for Girls,
The Works of Milton, nicely bound,
a tattered Atlas
(lands still shown in pink).
Tom Brown's Schooldays –
Decline and Fall?

Donkey

Seen on TV during the Balkans War

No carrots now, or sticks,
no water pail, no byre,
only an acrid smell
and rubble where the hawthorn grew.

No familiar word
or flick across the rump
only a brutal shove
with the butt-end of a gun.

And after limping through the shards
to seek a meadow or a stream
this old grey herbivore
is puzzled to find the water foul,
and, bedded in sweet grass,
decaying flesh and splintered bone.

Poem for Croatia
November, 1991

I watch the screen. The camera roams.
Dubrovnik. Split. A village with an ominous name
under a perfect azure sky.
I see the broken column in a classic square,
the smashed geranium in its shattered pot,
palace and pigsty equally undone –
Agree this is most democratic rape.

And as I watch, courtesy of high-tech art,
a mediaeval bell-tower crumbles,
a Roman temple cracks,
(last summer on those steps
the tourists posed for snaps).
Smoke hangs sullen over Tito's harvest fields
and over shifting seas where once
the pale Venetians sailed.

Can't bear to watch. Can't bear to turn away.
Voice-over talks of bombs, grenades and shells,
a ward of wounded children,
shell-shocked masses herded underground.

What do they think, the children,
                    with only tears to drink,
now Daddy's gone, and Granny's lost her mind,
and Mummy weeps and little sister's maimed?
and politicians talk and cease-fires fail to hold,
and age-old hatreds split the marriage bed?

We Europeans (who have seen it all before):
 "Such ancient wrongs, my dear,
 such bloody scores to settle –"
ponder which sphere of influence to back this time.

Another voice, an echo in my head:
 "Come with me, love, and we shall lie
 where sand and rocks and forest kiss the sea,
 beside the shining Adriatic."

But now on screen we see a map no logic can explain
fade to a tree inconsequently felled,
its blameless branches torn to hide the barrel of a gun.
Humanity is squatting like a toad.

I clear the screen.
The fading image cracks in schizophrenic pain.

O Dubrovnik.

Who's the betrayer? Who has been betrayed?
Forgive us, as we forgive you.

Refugee

Leave roof and rosebush,
rafters hung with herbs
leave wedding chest,
and children's toys,
the bed where they were born.

Leave folded linen,
quilt and woven rug
cups and kettle and coffee pot
and grandma's favourite chair.

Leave books and breadboard,
polished pans and painted plate,
window lace and ticking clock
and warm bricks round the hearth.

The stair that creaked,
the door that jammed
– they'll not trouble you again.

Chase the cat into the woods
open the birdcage,
let the linnet fly.
Lock the door
and throw away the key.

Pick up your bundle.
Go.

Feathers Don't Deny the Fur

After the first frantic fluttering
the bird hangs limp in the cat's jaw,
just as the mouse lies quiet in talons of the owl.
Heart still beating,
the open eye still sees the branches and the sky.

It does not struggle
because it knows the law
that from birth this driven fate must be
to make survival happen:
its own or any other's –
this little death has dignity.

The Fox

The fields are left behind, the woods recede,
and over the upland streaks the fox.
He's given them a run, and now
outstrips the frenzied jaws, the tearing teeth;
finds a lair, and sleeps, and takes his time
to saunter home beneath the moon.

Over the fields, stealthy, creeps the fox,
knows exactly when to freeze or pounce, and now
with prize held delicately in his teeth,
keeping appetite in check, in his own good time,
trots dutifully home beneath the moon
to sandy den where hunger can recede.

But fields are fewer, woods are scarcer now,
and so he'll hunt in barn or coop with eager teeth,
if choice is wide he'll take his time
and leave a trail of havoc beneath the moon
where the concrete spreads and woods recede.
Adapt and Live is the motto of the fox.

He's cunning, cautious, sharp of brain and teeth,
he's pulled a trick or twenty in his time,
he'll cross the motorway beneath the moon
to raid the rubbish tip, and then in shadows he'll recede,
pad smartly homeward, this resourceful fox –
a roadside culvert houses his cubs now.

A streetwise cub grows old before his time
– On urban lawns he's scavenged beneath the moon –
but does the memory of autumn fields recede
or shiver still beneath his russet pelt of fox?
Does this half-starveling dream that he yet now
steps lightly through the dew
                    with flesh between his teeth?

One night he'll be alone beneath the moon.
He'll learn that moonlight,
hunger, cold and even pain recede.
He's learned that some things never change for fox
except the klaxon hunting horn is louder now
and whirling wheels and streaking steel have teeth.
Even for fox the luck runs out some time.

The fields are left behind, the woods recede.

Agrigento
for Tom

These chiselled stones were old
when Jesus walked in Galilee –
temples built for wilder gods,
each column in imitation of the tree
that stood in the sacred grove.

"If you should go to Sicily," you'd said,
"above all things you must see Agrigento."
And you told me of the sense
of homecoming you'd felt
on that mystery-scattered ridge.

And so I clambered over rock
and placed my hand on golden stone,
made my reverence to Hera and to Zeus
gave thanks to Demeter and Kore
and smiled at Concord's harmony.

But mostly I wondered
if you too had put your hand
on that particular weathered stone,
or stood perhaps upon that very rock
where purple thyme beneath my feet
released its sharpening scent
to the honey-flavoured air.

After Giotto

In Padua, beneath the chapel's starry vault,
I marvel at Giotto's painted walls
illumined with the grief and grace
of human sorrow and the human face,
and, looking, think I understand
how after Giotto nothing was the same.
But near me another woman stands,
pale, plump, well past her middle age,
who looks and looks and faintly frowns
as if at a puzzle that she couldn't solve ...

I see her next in Salzburg,
sitting just across the aisle
while Mozart's music soars and sings,
and when applause rings thunderously out
I notice that she sits quite still,
hands clasped, head bowed, as if to pray.
She nods towards me as we leave
and I realise her cheeks are wet ...

Next time it's in Paris that we meet,
browsing among bookstalls by the Seine.
I turn and see her standing at my side,
as one by one she's drawing down
Dante from the crowded shelf,
then Shakespeare, Voltaire, Goethe, Hume,
gently holds them, weighs them in her hand,
only to replace them with a sigh.

                                        ...

She moves away, and as she goes
she looks at me and whispers slow and clear,
    "And yet, and yet ... ?"

And now she's with me everywhere I go
although I have not seen her face again,
in thought, in action even love's embrace;
because that last time, in Paris, as she walked away
she turned and slowly raised her hand,
and as she raised her hand her sleeve dropped back.
Her sleeve dropped back
and I could clearly see
        the number tattooed on her pale arm.

The Lake at Dawn

for my parents

The silence is holy,
the lake a black mirror
reflecting in its glassy surface
mountains, trees.

From round the point a pair of swans
glide along the far side of the lake
and slowly pass, until they reach
a distant reed-bed.

Only when the swans are out of sight
a slow smooth ripple
moves across the water
from the further shore
and laps the stones beneath my feet.

St Wolfgangsee, April 2011

WHODUNNIT?

Who killed the robin?
"Not I," said the farmer.
"My sprays and my muscles
my grubbed-up green hedges
had nothing to do with it
- the cold killed the robin."

Who blinded the baby?
"Not us," said the smoke-stacks.
"Our belch and our billow
may look pretty hellish,
but our toxic emissions
are simply not proven
to do any damage –
we've experts to say so
- shut up or we'll sue you."

Who drowned the villages,
flooded the delta?
"Act of God" said the loggers
remote in the mountains.
"Our State needs the timber,
without it we'd founder.
Your floods and erosion
are none of our business."

Who caused the young squaddy
to die of leukaemia?
"Not us," said the War Lords
in Whitehall's smooth fortress.
"He was merely detailed
to observe an explosion.
Precautions were taken
and overalls issued.
It's rotten bad luck
that so many have joined him,
but forty years later
it's really quite natural."

Who's to blame for the wreck
that blackens the beaches,
deals unspeakable death
in the wake of disaster?
"Not us," say the crew.
"We act on instructions."
"Not us," say the Owners.
"No laws have been broken."

Who sold the guns?
And who ruined the land?
(Drifting dust can reply.)
The starved child in the sand
 – who saw him die?
"I," said the fly,
"as I crawled on his eye –
   I saw him die."

For Hazel Goodsir Smith

Tomorrow I will pull myself together,
life will go on again.
But today,
today is yours
and I remember you,
seeing again
your smile of welcome
at the open door,
the warming dram
and oatcakes on a rosy plate,
delft tiles round the hearth,
the kist of logs.

How you loved your view of trees,
white tulips in a blue jug,
your purring cat,
the photos of your dear ones
so close at hand.

Books and paintings were your friends
and Highland Mary on the shelf,
a wally dug or two,
and all the small mementos
of a love so great
that years dissolved away
as, sharing memories,
you became again
the laughing girl
who made a poet sing.

The Visiting Hour
for my brother, Colin, 1939 – 1986

Beyond the iron gate
a spread of golden roses
bordered the path
from the road to Ward 16.

And daily on my way
to keep that summer vigil
beside your frozen bed
I watched one special bud unfold,
seeing your furled childhood
in that green protective clasp.

And day by day,
watching the rose unfolding
lifting its face towards the life-giving sun
its sturdy stock deep rooted in warm earth,
I remembered your boyhood's grace and strength,
your hopes, your certainties,
the glowing energy of your youth.

And for a day the rose
at its nooning time
opened its heart
to hold the image of the sun,
until a bitter wind shook down
those vivid petals one by one,
to fall like teardrops
to the welcoming earth.

Memento Mori

for Michael Levy

A simple notice
stating date and place.
A sudden jolt.
A name unspoken for a lifetime.
Too late now for flowers,
and anyway we did not part as friends.
So why the shock?

Stop it.
Stop the tape.
Don't spool back now
to jokes and rows,
a thatch of hair,
a wicked laugh.

Fifty years have done their work.
Look in the mirror.

Who's next?

On Not Having Grandchildren

I would have waited for your coming
in fear and exultation,
gripped your mother's hand and wiped her brow,
knitted you a magic shawl
to shield you from all harm,
lulled you to sleep with songs my mother sang.

Your chubby portrait in a silver frame
would have made me smile
each time I looked at it,
searching for family likeness
in your beaming face.

Later, if allowed, I would have read you stories,
given you books,
taken you to concerts, shown you art.

I would have taught you the names
of wild flowers and birds,
cooked apple crumble for you when you came to stay,
listened to your grievances and hopes,
tried to explain how life is beautiful
though not always fair.

Among the other grannies I'd have held my own,
unequalled in tales of beauty, cleverness and skill,
amazed that one so young could be so smart.

Child of my imaginings, you live only in my heart –
but, safe as the kernel in a nut, I keep you there.

The Three Mothers

for Torin, Amber, Liane and Marina

Little ones,
you have three mothers:
The mother who longed for you, bore you,
formed your limbs,
pushed you out into the waiting world
with a cry of pain and joy.

Your second mother's love
is anchored to the other
united in a bond of trust
and pride in you.

You have a third mother, Nature,
who holds the world between her hands,
creates the furled leaf and spreading oak,
nurtures imagination and the human skill –
whose alchemy produced
the miracle of your birth.

These are your mothers.
Listen to their voices,
respect their powers and their fragilities.
Love them and heed their words.

Quartet
for Tom

I

I never knew from what wild spring,
what overflowing fountain,
this fall of water came –
only knew it held me there
on some high ledge
transfixed between its liquid crystal
and the rock –
sometimes a sparkling, starry veil
of rainbow spray and splintered light
and droplets you could sprinkle from your hand,
sometimes a black and terrifying wall
of rush and roar
no-one would dare touch.

On and on it flowed
this surge and gush,
singing in summer spate,
crackling under winter's jagged ice,
but always flowing, nourishing green fronds,
carving a way through rock.
And then quite suddenly it stopped.

I feel the stone dry at my back
and see the dizzying drop beneath my feet.

II

Silent as snowflakes
petals drift down.
Looking up through softly laden branches
I see blue sky.
Somewhere a blackbird
is calling to his mate.
All around are signs that spring is here.
But you are not.
The snow is falling on a hard ground.

III

Sitting alone in a pub
on the shady side of the street,
through the window pane I saw
the shadow of a huge bird
swoop over the roof
and down the sunlit wall
of the house on the other side.
The shadow did not touch the ground
but sailed up again and vanished.
Just for a moment,
through a play of light,
reality and unreality were one:
And finally I knew
beyond the shadow of a doubt
your spirit had flown clear
of this dark Platonic cave.

IV

When will I cease to see you
stalking through the crowd –
the spring of hair,
the set of the shoulder,
the slow familiar stride –
Instinctively I move to greet
your known smile,
your blue gaze,
and meet instead a stranger's face?

Old Lady's Hands

These hands once curled
around a mother's finger,
then learned to lift a cup
to hold a pen
to sew a seam
to trace the outline
of a lover's cheek
to cradle a baby's head
to bind a wound
to prune a rose.

These hands, once so busy,
now lie still,
and wait for the blessing
of another's touch.

The Glass Hammer

Words are weapons
We both know how to use.
Sometimes it's the flick-knife
That we choose,
Sometimes the heavy claymore,
Or a dagger to the heart.

Sometimes it's you
Sometimes it's me
Who gasping, wounded, lies.

But why is it when I've hurt you
I'm the one who cries?

The Visitor

Just about this time,
in the eleventh hour
of the last night
of the dying year,
when the last wan leaf
would shatter the frozen silence
with its fall,

You listen for the footstep
on the stair,
wait to embrace the empty air,
and lift your lips
to kiss the wolf-snarl of the past.

Translations from the Italian
by Heather Scott

Giuseppe Ungaretti

Eternal

Eterno

Between the flower that is gathered
                and the one that is given
the inexpressible nothing

Detachment

Distacco

Here is a man
like any other

Here is a soul
deserted
like an unreflecting mirror

I sometimes wake up
and gather myself
and possess

The rare gift that is born for me
is born for me so quietly

Which when its time is past
just as imperceptibly passes away

Lindoro of the Desert

Lindoro di deserto

A hovering of wings in mist
breaks the silence of the eyes

The wind unfurls the rose
of a thirst of kisses

I weaken at dawn

My life spills over me
in a whirl of nostalgia

Now I mirror the corners of the world
that I have travelled
and I know them by their scent

Until death at the mercy of the journey

We have the respite of sleep

The sun dries up the tears

I cover myself in a warm cloak
of gold

From this ledge of desolation
I hold out my arms
to embrace
the warmth of the day

In Memoriam

His name was
Moammed Sceab

Descendant
of emirs of nomads
he killed himself
because he no longer had
a Homeland

He loved France
and changed his name

He was Marcel
but he was not French
and could no longer
live
in the tent of his people
where one hears the murmured chant
of the Koran
while sipping coffee

And he did not know how
to release
the song
of his loneliness

I went with him
together with the landlady
of our lodgings in Paris
from number 5 rue des Carmes
a shabby run-down alley

He lies
in the cemetery of Ivry
a suburb where
it always seems
the day
of dismantling a fair

And perhaps only I
still know
that he lived

San Martino del Carso

Valley of the Solitary Tree, 27 August, 1916

Of these houses
nothing remains
but a few
scraps of wall

Of so many
men like me
remains
not even that much

But in my heart
not one lacks a cross

My heart
is the land
more devastated

Italy

I am a poet
a unanimous cry
I am a particle of dreams

I am a fruit
of countless diverse graftings
ripened in a hot-house

But your People are carried
by the same earth
that carries me
Italy

In this uniform
a soldier of yours
I take my rest
as if in the cradle
of my father

Nostalgia

When
night is giving way to dawn
just before the coming of spring
and people
seldom pass

Over Paris there thickens
a sombre colour
of grief

In a corner
of a bridge
I contemplate
the infinite silence
of a slender girl

Our sufferings
unite

And as though carried elsewhere
we are still there

The Buried Harbour

Il Porto Sepolto

The poet comes among us
and then turns to the light with his songs
and scatters them there

Of this poetry
I remember only
that nothingness
of infinite secrecy

Giuseppe Ungaretti, 1888-1970, born Alexandria, Egypt, into a family from Lucca, Tuscany. Modernist poet, journalist, essayist, critic, academic, civil servant. Served in the trenches during World War 1. These translations were published in Like Leaves in Autumn, *responses to the war poetry of Giuseppe Ungaretti, ed Carlo Pirozzi and Katherine Lockton, Luath Press, 2015.*

Roberto Sanesi

Sometimes They Pass Swiftly
and Mysteriously

Passano a volte rapidi e non si sa che fare

'because if the name were a form, only a sort
of assignment, we would know nothing'

Sometimes they pass swiftly, sketching
hints, farewells, vegetations
that creep towards the *Stimmung*: what
senses the duration, the dimension
of the names in the coming time?
They quiver.
They pretend to explain themselves.
In the stretches where they pause bounded
by the invisible limits of a too-long sleep
there are still signs.
All the colours and the beds of autumn.
The uncompleted spring on the other side.
And shapes gathered in the gardens.
Or maybe a faint sound, a forsaking
of places that shift and change
without the light ever
flowing backwards in the urgent need
to reaffirm itself. Sometimes
one imagines that they exist.

The Grindstone of the Sea

La macina del mare

If the sea, its expanse, if the sea,
the grindstone of the sea, the roar
of the tide that surges and withdraws,
the luminous water, endless archipelago
of beacons of abandoned boats, if the sea
under the keel of trees, and gulfs, blossoming
waves that surface at the sound, dazzled, driftwoods
from my wreckage, and the clouds, and all
that plunges, desert of blue,
if the sea,
things seen and heard in mysteries,
the return and the starting point that govern,
the sunset that opens the horizon, the guardian
of all gardens, calmness and change, the flame
of air, the transit, the mirror,
the vague imitation of oneself, the embrace
of the deep, the void and the fathoming
of necessity, even further, further away in the place
that grows more distant, in the whiteness, in the centre,
if the sea,
the thought of the sea emerges out of sleep,
astoundingly the outline
of all things unites, the design, the earth,
suddenly
in bounded limits are limitless.

Lake Thun, from Life I

Lago di Thun dal vero, I

Guage the distance, close your eyes, the lake
    lives on quietly, takes shape.
But its vesperal knowledge,
its closeness to the light, to the trees,
requires deliberate brewing of a storm, lightning
that splits the mountain in two, the sinking
wreck and the wild crosswind, the shore
lashed with rain, the sudden crack
lost among the trees, and the shriek, the sail
shredded by a ghostly whirlwind.
    Only in this way can we understand
the exact relation between the waters and the void.

The First Day of Spring

Il primo giorno di primavera

Something that someone
will do afresh again and again,
unconsciously. The innocence
of this moisture,
the hidden identity of the monologue,
and the usual rustling
that rises in the trees, the bones
fallen from the moon.
On this enclosure.
With the blackness of snails in the undergrowth.
With the night-time springing of green shoots
the whole length of the meadow.

And maybe the archangel of sand.
But then you have made something
of this symmetry.
It is this.
And the voice that calls across
from one bank to another.
And names who separate.
And those who stroke each other's brows.
But who, why, in what way
are you threatening me?
With the withering clods of earth.
With the figures that pass by lightly dressed
along a path we do not even know.
Well, I defy it: but then
simply the rain,
the cause, the effect,
its demonstration.
This land inhabited
by imperceptible sounds.

No Date

Senza data

Why carry things to a conclusion
when no one, in the garden,
has ever seen my wisteria cease to be.
If then the flower were to fail,
this, we would say, is the beauty of the world,
its visible experience.

Song (for Federico)

Canzone (per Federico)

With a face of a hare
with the shoes of the moon
when she takes two steps down
into the frost of winter
while the air thins
in the fragile tracery
when she speaks and does not answer
when she makes out of mud
the legends of light
within the eyes and the roots
when she scrapes out in the loam
the limits of the night
with triangle and hoes
when she eavesdrops behind the wall
for the memory of a bud
that flowers in the thought
with discordant voices
of depth and height
where fire is a yearning
that opens and closes the horizon.
He knows that on the surface
there is no green, the dream is lacking.
Beauty hides
within a sound, a sound, a sound ...

Classification

Verifica

Eternity never lasts long.
Things are simple, and so
why speak, or write. The effect
of nature is noble and nonsensical.
It is motionless. It recurs.
He thought all night of the names of the morning.
The night caught fire on a sickle
that danced furiously in the middle of the corn.
Be that as it may.
He said it is cold green invisible: yet
earth, memories it is early listen come
(And if there were no other substance
what use would its description be).
Fleeting persistence, my dear
form of displacement, as you see
the mountain is intact.

Roberto Sanesi, 1930-2001, born Milan, Italy. Poet, translator, editor, academic, teacher, art critic and publisher. These translations were published in The First Day of Spring, *ed Mattco Brera, Troubador Publishing, 2014. The last two are taken from 'seven unpublished poems', in the same volume.*

Dante Marianacci

Squalls and Dizziness

Vento e Vertigini

Unfurl the sails
of your wondering thoughts
and follow the drift
of distant memories.
And do not linger
only in rose garden of dreams
that have strewn
your path
with squalls and dizziness.
Every time the games
seemed over
a storm blew up
and swept away the wreckage.
To build a house on water
was like casting smiles
into the darkness of the night.

It is a Hard Passage

È un Transito Pesante

It is a hard passage through
the time of memories you told me
you who more than I
used to halt at the barrier of goodbyes.
Perhaps it still sustains us
a stifled cry of hope.

This man who dreams of domination
who doesn't give a damn for what men say
who can't begin to understand our griefs
he will see the stars grow fainter
one by one
and the sky grow dark above his head.

He will see pass before his eyes
the confessed criminal of carelessness
the madness of the fraudster
always in retrospect with hope.

The Poets Post Mortem

I poeti post mortem

A drunken man came in
and recited four lewd verses.
At the fifth
someone thought to throw him out.
They did the same
at yet another pub.
And then in yet another.
Until at last they'd chased him
from all the howffs in the city.
Now they compete for his memory
by way of plaques upon the walls.
"He came here to pass some happy hours."
It is the fate of poets
that they achieve such lustre
always after dying.

Other Heroes

Altri Eroi

The passionate singer
of the candle in the wind
who jolts the heart
is not the greater tongue
of ancient flame
who in his lifetime
navigated other seas
to learn the secrets of the world.
Earth has bred other heroes,
new mythologies
digitally generated.

Between the Musician and the Poet

Tra il musico e il poeta

Perhaps Wagner was right.
Between the musician and the poet
the distance is unbridgeable at times
and the form of the melody
is richer than that
of the symphony.
Immerse yourself therefore without fear
in the deep ocean
of your music.
And I will lead you by the hand
and give order to your chaos

because all is no longer all
in this world of mythographers
and usurpers
of Siegfrieds and Fisher Kings
of little Fausts and puppets
of Nobel winners who do not bow.

The Fate of Dreams

Il Destino dei Sogni

In the great house built long ago
you too, like Stevenson,
arranged five tables,
one for every room.

On each one mountains
of books, except for one
desolately bare.

But there by now
you rarely sit
and the pages remain unwritten.

The fate of dreams
is to vanish before the dawn.

Dante Marianacci, b 1948, poet, novelist, translator, editor, Director of Italian Institutes in various countries, including Edinburgh. These translations are taken from Signori dei Vento, Lords of the Wind, *EDIZIONI NOUBS, 2002 and from Heather's own typescript.*

Biographical Note

Heather Scott (née Fretwell) was born in London in 1935. At the onset of the Blitz she was evacuated first to North Wales and then to Scotland. Both experiences made a deep impression on her and her first serious poem, written at age 8 for a school magazine, was entitled 'The Trossachs'!

She left school early at 16 to care for a sick mother and a younger brother. She had always loved English and French at school but had few qualifications. Determined to continue her education, she earned some money doing little typing jobs locally, and when free to do so went to France, enrolling at the Sorbonne for a year to do a course in French Civilisation. She gained her Diploma and then got a job as a typist in the Organisation for European Economic Co-operation in Paris.

In 1969, she moved to Edinburgh and applied to do a degree in French and English at the University. There she met and married the poet, editor and critic Tom Scott, a socialist and passionate upholder of the Scots language, which at that time was not a politically approved position.

With an unworldly husband and a young family, Eric, and Kim and Marina, twins, all born within a short space of time, Heather soon became the breadwinner, and worked for years as a teacher in an Edinburgh City primary school. Over and above that, she was highly engaged in a range of different interests, cultural and political, active in the Labour Party, and later for the Scottish National Party.

After retiring, she studied Italian and translated several collections of Italian poetry, including Giuseppe Ungaretti, Roberto Sanesi and Dante Marianacci. Her own articles and poetry appeared occasionally in Scottish publications such as *The Scotsman*, *Gambit*, *Scotia Review* and *Chapman*.

On Reading Heather's Poems ...

Heather Scott's poetry is bound to the diurnal, the familiar, though she is eloquent too on 'high-flown themes'. Her depictions of personal tragedies are permeated with warmth and humanity, and alongside cries of loss and longing are moments of stillness and tension, as in visiting the Giotto frescoes in Padua, or describing a hunted fox under moonlight. Her natural poetic rhythms ring true: homely but never couthy, and without any hint of portentousness or affectation.

Stewart Conn

In this fine collection, the poems range widely both in location and theme, touching on love and domestic life, but the concerns of the world are never far below the surface. Whether writing of war and refugees, art or religion, human disappointment or joy, her pen is empathetic. Her language and imagery can be sensual and tender, or sharp and polemical; but always she displays a fine attention to the rhythms and sound resonances of language which adds to the pleasure of reading this book.

Christine de Luca

Her poems are an astonishment: tense, incredibly tough and resilient, yet hypersensitive readings of reality, showing that work composed by a woman can be unconfined and undefined by gender. Yet the place of perception, the understanding, is distinctly feminine, giving the poems strengths and distinction as moving statements of love and comradeship and of essential human worth. There is never a false note, a misjudged tone. The need for shelter, the waste of wars as refugees flee, as children, women, and animals die, and the virtues of art, the paintings of Giotto, all testify to Heather Scott's enduring openness to the world, her engagement with its joys and griefs,

70

from the lasting 'wolf-snarl of the past' to what the future still has to yield to the living and the unborn yet to come.

Alan Riach

In the poem 'Iona', a confessional, of the questioning faith presented by his colleagues, St Columba predicts that in time his brothers' scepticism will be "shriven white as the stones upon this beach". This also applies in Heather Scott's poetry. At first, the beguiling simplicity can seem "bleak and bare", but there is "sweet water in the rocks" to be found. The absolution she seeks isn't critical acclaim or the plaudits of peers, but simply to share her wonder "in this place of earth".

Asif Khan

This harvest of over half a century of Heather Scott's poetry, came to me as a very happy surprise. Her poems have accessibility, melody and the feeling of being completely necessary utterances. Here we have some of the core subjects of all great literature – love, loss, family and home, and her finely sensitive translations of Giuseppe Ungaretti, Roberto Sanesi and Dante Marianacci. With the publication of *After Giotto* her work will get at last the attention and validation it richly deserves.

Richie McCaffery

I am Heather's friend since we both tried to learn Italian in the Italian Institute in Edinburgh. The poems touch me deeply, as I feel close to her through them. We went together to Italy together for several years and we found traces of Tom's stay in Agrigento years before: - Heather's joy was something to behold! Our adventures there linger unforgettably in my memory. I didn't know she had so many sometimes very personal poems on the great moments in her life, but think that the shocks, the pain - and the happiness of it all - have found their way into these truly impressive poems.

Ingrid Kimbell

The Top Board

What! dive from there! My dear, I couldn't!
For a thousand pounds I wouldn't.
The very thought gives me the shivers,
I'll leave that board for higher divers,
The dangers seem to me too great,
And I my limbs appreciate.
Supposing, as I perched up there,
Far from the ground, high in the air,
Losing balance I quickly dropped
And just suppose I belly-flopped!
Or into someone else dived slap and
Broke my neck – such things have happened.
The board's too high, the steps are steep
And people stop to watch one leap:
I don't think I will ever dare
To have the pluck to dive from there!

Heather Fretwell (Lower VJ)

Wimbledon High School Magazine
(Girls Public Day School Trust)
No 57, May 1950